Melodies From Within
a collection in verse

by

Leesa A. Wheeler

authorHOUSE™

1663 LIBERTY DRIVE, SUITE 200
BLOOMINGTON, INDIANA 47403
(800) 839-8640
WWW.AUTHORHOUSE.COM

First published by AuthorHouse 05/20/05

ISBN: 1-4208-3833-4 (sc)

Printed in the United States of America
Bloomington, Indiana

This book is printed on acid-free paper.

Poetry by Leesa A. Wheeler
Several Selections of poetry by Leesa A. Wheeler and Patsy W. Hale
Cover design by Leesa A. Wheeler
Graphics by Karen Lawson

Melodies from Within
a collection in verse

Date ~ _____

For ~ _____

On the Occasion of ~ _____

From ~ _____

"Talk to yourself like you'd like others to talk to you.
Treat yourself like you'd like to be treated."
Words to live by from Leesa and Bella

This book is lovingly dedicated to

R. W. "Buck" Wheeler, Jr.

My Daddy

A guiding light in my life

Thanks To...

My Heavenly Father and my Lord and Savior, Jesus Christ ~ words cannot express the thankfulness in my heart for you. Thank you for your presence, prayers, plans, power, provision, protection and peace in my life daily. Every step of the way you've helped me grow ~ For You, is the glory forever! My parents, Buck and Ida Wheeler, who inspired me, encouraged me, & instilled in me the confidence to reach for my dreams! My sister, Patsy, with whom I share the journey of sisterhood & life~for sharing the joy of writing! My beloved Bella, my charming companion! Trish and Christie, "my little sisters," how special you are! Rebecca, your intuition is incredible! Judy, who tells me what I need to hear! Janet, for your creativity and our special spiritual moments! Yvette, who showed me the joy of laughing at myself! Mary, your encouragement is always on time! Jennifer, Philip, Shane~you've always been there. Your friendship is treasured! Melissa, for sharing your canine knowledge ~ because of you, I'm a better dog mother! All who have crossed my path~my life is richer for having known you. You, the reader, I pray that these words from my heart will touch yours.

Author's Proem
"my prelude"

The poems in this collection are a compilation of my life experiences. During my life I've found my most memorable moments have been blessings discovered from facing challenges. Each heart has a song to sing. Have a seat, relax, and listen to the songs of my heart... perhaps you'll be reminded of the songs in yours.

Leesa

Table of Contents

Seasonal Selections

Awakening

Sunrays stream light and warmth to all it touches
Squirrels scurry in a game of chase
New life springs forth after slumber

Dew dances on grass blades as diamonds glitter
Gray mist envelopes the surroundings like a babe in a blanket
Tears of joy fall to refresh and quench life's thirst

Tree limbs outstretched toward Heaven
Gnarled and twisted, yet peaceful and serene
A robin sings to babes in her nest
Water gently rolls and splashes over rocks in its path
On it's way to a final destination.

Summer Stroll

Crisp caresses from a cool morning breeze
Oh, the aroma of freshly cut grass
Strong old oaks offer shade and a cool retreat from the scorching sun
The wind fondles leaves as they dance to the melody of life
While fireflies as flickering flames gleam in the evening air.

Autumn Arrival

Leaves falling in the streetlamp's glow
Appear as twinkling stars in the night
Listening to rustling, crunching echoes
While waltzing through the fallen leaves
Sounds of a rhythmic symphony linger till dawn
Earth's crisp cool breath tingles the flesh
Warmth shared from a fire-fueled embrace
As crackling timber's flames quench its thirst.

Winter Walk

Ice crackles beneath my steps as I withdraw to warmth and comfort
Tree limbs now stripped and barren, completely exposed
Iced tears drop like daggers, piercing the earth
Snowflakes, each different, yet lost in a crowd
Quiet and still, frozen for a moment in time.

Holiday and Special Occasion Selections

♪♫

We Give Thanks

On this Thanksgiving Day, we praise the Lord above,
For His many blessings and the depth of His great love.

Ours has been a blessed life, one full of mercy and care,
Thankful are we for the opportunity to come to You in prayer.
We thank You especially today, that You are with us everywhere!

God, You've blessed us as a family for many years,
You've been beside us through the laughter and the tears.
We have treasured memories that will never die,
Our family loves You deeply, there are so many reasons why.

The eternal life given us by God, we fill with joy to embrace,
For all we are and possess, we are given by His grace.
Thank you, oh our Father, for sending us your Son,
For through His love and by His death the victory is won!

A Thankful Heart

I'm thankful for...
the sunrise and sunset, sun, moon and stars
breezes and shade
Bella
trusting God's Heart when I can't trace His Hand
my friends
my best friends
seasons of the year and their reflection of God's Glory
music
my life experiences
being able to read, write, talk and understand
the ocean, its beauty and melody
good books
all the foods I can eat
the Bible
water and iced green tea
my spiritual gifts
those who do for me what I cannot do for myself
the products I can use and the things I can do
my home ~ my safe haven
twinkle lights and fans
laughter and tears
Jesus, who saved and intercedes for me
treasured memories and splendid moments
answered prayers
the peace and joy I've experienced living with my limits
a God who knows me and loves me
the plans God has for me
gloves, socks, and a hat on a cold day
my health
God's healing in my life
God's peace, faithfulness, forgiveness, direction, control, protection,
provision, grace, mercy, love, and strength in my life daily
my mother and daddy, for their example of Godly parents,
their love, encouragement, strength, and stability in my life
my sister for her inspiration, love, listening, and being a best friend
those who stand in the gap for me.

Daddy's Girls

We are so lucky to have a father full of love,
A man who's the very likeness of our Father up above.
Daddy, you taught us right from wrong with loving guidance and advice.
You helped us walk our journey through life; No one else could suffice.

You've set an example of how to live right,
Follow God's pathway - The Truth and The Light.
With you as our father we truly delight,
We love you with all of our might.

It fills our hearts with joy and pride,
To let you know your deepest prayers are justified.
Our Lord is your Lord and he lives in our heart,
We want to thank you today for giving us our start.

It's our desire to follow the footsteps you've trod,
For you are our father, chosen by God.

Happy Father's Day!
Leesa A. Wheeler and Patsy W. Hale

My Daddy

As father and daughter we share a special bond of love,
One that's pure and true.
The most important man in my life?
Yes, Daddy, it's you!

There isn't a day when I haven't known your love,
Just like our Heavenly Father above.
Being your little girl brings happiness to me,
For the Best Father in the World, you're my nominee!

I'm a lot like you, Daddy, and I'm proud to say,
I wouldn't have it any other way.
That God chose you for me, I'm so thankful and blessed,
I love you more than words can express.

♪♫

Her Lord's Servant

A testimony of...
Your reflection of God's Love
Your devotion to your family
Your beauty
Your sacrificial living
Your joy in doing for others
Your heart for service
Your gentleness
Your compassion
Your knowing Jesus as Lord and Savior
Your desire to do His will
Your fruit-bearing service
Your willingness to be used by Him
Your faith and trust in God and His Sovereignty
Your relationship with The Father
God's Love for you
My love for you, my beloved Mother.

♪♫

Our Mother's Love

On this your special day, we praise the Lord above,
For the gentleness and depth of our dear Mother's love.
Ours has been a blessed life, a life of love and care,
All that you've ever had or wanted, you would always share.

The most fortunate of all children are Leesa and I.
We have a Mother for whom we would die.
Kindness, goodness and generosity are the qualities we see in you.
Our prayer is daily to possess them, too.

We're the two most thankful daughters on earth,
For God chose you to be the Mother of our birth.
We glorify our Lord for giving us you, a godly Mother,
For you are like none other.

You are the epitome of giving from the heart,
Nothing, no nothing, can tear us apart.

Happy Mother's Day!
Leesa A. Wheeler and Patsy W. Hale

Dear Mother

Being your daughter is a blessing in my life,
I hope I'll be like you one day,
Should I become a mother and a wife.

You taught me about Jesus and you've loved me since birth.
This has made me the happiest, richest woman on earth!

You've always been there for me, through thick and thin.
Mother, you know, you're my best friend!

You showed me the happiness of giving and doing for another,
I thank God every day that you are my mother.

I'm thankful, too, for your mother, Gan,
You followed in her footsteps and with God's help, I can.

♪♫

Our Daughter

A bundle of joy we couldn't wait to embrace,
In this world and in our hearts, you have a special place.
We're the most thankful parents on earth,
It's a blessed event for us, this your birth!

A precious little girl, God's chosen one for us,
Each moment spent with you, glorious!
A blessing for our family you will always be,
The arrival of you, our daughter, a treasured memory.

Our little girl, our heart's desire,
Our prayer for you, you'll become what you aspire.
You're a gift from Heaven placed in our arms today,
Our love for you, more than words can say.

Our Son

A bundle of joy we couldn't wait to embrace,
In this world and in our hearts, you have a special place.
We're the most thankful parents on earth,
It's a blessed event for us, this your birth!

God chose you for us, a precious little boy,
Each moment shared with you, one to enjoy
Our little son, our heart's desire,
Our prayer for you, you'll become what you aspire.

A blessing for our family you will always be,
The arrival of you, our son, a treasured memory.
You're a gift from Heaven placed in our arms today,
Our love for you, more than words can say.

Contemplation

Best Friends

An understanding not visible in words
Communication taking place with even a look or gesture
Sharing experiences
Openness and acceptance, laughter and tears
My confidante, close no matter how far
Forever friends, bonded in trust
Always forgiven, always loved.

Morning Glories

Light and warmth rise after slumber
As clarity abounds
Cries of sorrow, cries of joy
Even in tragedy, treasures evolve
Just as His word endures forever
So comes the dawn.

Reflection

Peering through the windows of my soul
Identical self ~ exposed
Always and never the same
Intricately woven layers of emotion ~ transparent
Still, an ensemble all my own.

♪♫

Splendid Moments

Reflections in time,
Memories of faces and places,
Treasures reunited,
Hearts and minds smiling from within.

Twinkles of joy and blessedness
Fill our lives.
Fragrances, sounds, sensations, and hues
All ours to savor.

Wonderful events seep into our being,
Recalled in an instant.
Embracing splendid moments,
Eagerly awaiting those still to come!

Foreign Hearts

A connection, so strong, so fast
Different cultures drawn to each other
Sparks of attraction, unexplainable.

A smile, a gaze, sounds of voices stir from within
Passion, subtle yet recognized, in the electric whisper of a touch
Anticipation of an encounter, two becoming one?

So alike, so opposite
Strong degrees of separation
Still bonded in desire and respect
Wondering, dreaming, togetherness in time?
Yet destined perhaps to remain at a distance.

♪♫

Eternity Bound

Living, not existing, until your turn arrives
The moment to occur unknown
Except by The Father
For some in the blink of an eye
For others, time for preparation
Leaving loved ones behind for a while
With promises and deeds fulfilled or ignored
A decision must be made
Acceptance or rejection of Jesus, the Lamb of God
Then, assured passage through the gateway ~ Heaven's peace or Hell's pain?
Your choice for your soul's residence
Your homecoming, a reunion of souls, all you've hoped for and more!
Minute by minute narrowing the gap for facing your eternity.

Sisters

An understanding not visible in words
Communication taking place with even a look or gesture
Sharing experiences
Openness and acceptance, laughter and tears
Confidantes, close no matter how far
Bonded in trust, a blessing from God
Inspirer, encourager, the very best of friends
Always forgiven, always loved.

Blessed Events

Streams of Love descend upon the faces of God's children
With evidence of Trust and Hope as emotions soar
Pain filtered by Joy as God's plan unfolds
Adapting in this life, while Peace blooms day by day.

♪♫

Grace Disguised

Invisible veil disappearing
Emotions exposed
Searing streams of tears welled from within
Weeping, wondering, understanding, and trusting
Yet, still a hurting heart
Longing for hugs and held hands
Listening for the sound of the voice
Peace provided only by The Lamb
My soul's source of calm comfort.

Breathe

A gentle rise and fall with each breath taken
The rhythm ~ personal, precious, priceless
Existence ~ essential
Expectations of your essence's caress
Emotions ~ expressed
Intimacy shared in quiet moments
With calm cessation, eternity's entered...

Daily Dilemma

What's it like to be me?
An illusion of health struggling to survive
Managing sensitive senses
Constantly changing allergens ~ inhaled and ingested
Smells and tastes turn toxic
Swollen, flushed face and limbs
Waves of heat, nausea, lightheadedness, fatigue, aches
Consequences experienced only by me

Constant concern ~ is it safe for me to breathe or eat?
Bombarded ~ no way to escape
Others oblivious ~ couldn't care less
Always alert ~ exhausted efforts take their toll
Private tears release frustration from isolation
Searching for a solution ~ a cure
The answer? avoid places ~ avoid people
Separated from daily and special events
Time silently stolen from family and friends
Wondering will this battle ever end?

Amidst this storm, bountiful blessings arrive
Special souls ~ once strangers ~ now friends
Compassion given for my limitations
Daily delivery of endurance with glimpses given of vitality
Faith, trust, hope ~ my constant companions
Intricately woven into the unfinished tapestry of me
Until He heals me, won't you understand?
What it's like to be me...

Charming Companions

With her gentle expression of love, I began each day smiling
Awakened by chimes of joy around her neck
Tail wagging, she entered my room
A morning kiss ~ the tender touch of her nose on my face

Our communication ~ a language all its own
Beside beloved Brandy as she took her last breath
My aching heart cried out ~ her peace ~ my pain
Wondering, would I ever love another?

Searching, I soon found her ~ Una Isabella De La Sol

Awakened by the chimes of joy as she awakes
Snorting, tail wagging, she arrives bedside
We snuggle ~ Bella's paws tucked under or over my arm
Many morning kisses ~ the tender touch of her nose on my face

Training together, constant companions sharing a special bond
Complete understanding, unconditional love, and trust
Our communication ~ a language all our own
With her enduring expression of love, I begin each day smiling.

In Memory Of...

His Lord's Servant

A testimony of...
Your love for God
Your love for Puddin, Patsy, and me
Your love for your friends
Your tears of joy and thankfulness
Your faith and trust in God and His Sovereignty
Your peace in His will
Your strength from God
Your relationship with The Father
Your teaching His word
Your knowing Jesus as Lord and Savior
Your faithful service
Your willingness to be used by Him
Your living and leading by example
Your life spent seeking the Master's face
God's love for you
Our love for you, Our beloved Father.

In love and memory of my Beloved Daddy,
R. W. "Buck" Wheeler, Jr.
1920~2001

Introducing Leesa's website ~ www.HealthyHighway.org

Welcome to a NEW way of living...

www.HealthyHighway.org was created as a resource/reference guide for those like me who suffer from allergies, have experienced the death of a loved one, and those who want the best for their dog. For those of you who don't have allergies, you'll find plenty of information for you too! Visit often as we are always adding new products and services. We hope you will discover something that helps you live your best life!

About the Author

Photograph by Eric Nelson

Leesa lives in Georgia with her beloved Bella.

Invitation to participate in Leesa's upcoming
book ~ <u>Charming Companions</u>

Leesa's currently at work on another publication, Charming Companions. To contribute to Leesa's upcoming book, Charming Companions, send a digital photo of you and your pet along with a paragraph or two as to why he/she is your charming companion to CharmingCompanions@yahoo.com. Those selected and included in this publication will receive a complimentary copy of the book. She anticipates completion in fall 2006.

Printed in the United States
31888LVS00003B/461